Backpack Books
122 Fifth Avenue
New York, NY 10011

ISBN 0-7607-7188-X

Manufactured in Thailand for Hall Associates, Inc.

05 06 07 08 09 MCH 10 9 8 7 6 5 4 3 2 1

The 12 Days of Christmas

Illustrated by Alison Julian

BACK**PACK**BOOKS
·
NEW YORK

On the first day of Christmas, my true love sent to me
a partridge in a pear tree.

On the second day of Christmas, my true love sent to me
two turtle doves,

and a partridge in a pear tree.

On the third day of Christmas, my true love sent to me
three French hens,

two turtle doves, and a partridge in a pear tree.

On the fourth day of Christmas, my true love sent to me
four calling birds,

three French hens, two turtle doves, and a partridge in a pear tree.

On the fifth day of Christmas, my true love sent to me
five golden rings,

four calling birds, three French hens, two turtle doves, and a partridge in a

pear tree.

On the sixth day of Christmas, my true love sent to me

six geese a-laying,

five golden rings, four calling birds, three French

hens, two turtle doves, and a partridge in a pear tree.

On the seventh day of Christmas, my true love sent to me

seven swans a-swimming,

six geese a-laying, five golden rings, four

calling birds, three French hens, two turtle doves, and a partridge in a pear tree.

On the eighth day of Christmas, my true love sent to me
eight maids a-milking,

seven swans a-swimming, six geese a-laying, five golden rings, four calling birds, three French

hens, two turtle doves, and a partridge in a pear tree.

On the ninth day of Christmas, my true love sent to me *nine ladies dancing,*

eight maids a-milking, seven swans a-swimming, six geese a-laying, five golden rings, fou

calling birds, three French hens, two turtle doves, and a partridge in a pear tree.

On the tenth day of Christmas, my true love sent to me
ten lords a-leaping,

nine ladies dancing, eight maids a-milking, seven swans a-swimming, six geese a-laying,

...ve golden rings, four calling birds, three French hens, two turtle doves, and a partridge in a pear tree.

On the eleventh day of Christmas, my true love sent to me

eleven pipers piping,

ten lords a-leaping, nine ladies dancing, eight maids a-milking, seven swans a-swimming, six geese a-laying,

ve golden rings, four calling birds, three French hens, two turtle doves, and a partridge in a pear tree.

On the twelfth day of Christmas, my true love sent to me
twelve drummers drumming,

nine ladies dancing, eight maids a-milking, seven swans a-swimming, six geese

eleven pipers piping, ten lords a-leaping,

...laying, five golden rings, four calling birds, three French hens, two turtle doves, and a partridge in a pear tree.